HAMLYN · COLOURFAX · SERIES

S.P.I.E.S
and codes

A. N. AGENT

CONTENTS

HAMLYN

WHAT IS A SPY?

A spy is someone who finds out secret information and passes it on to another person. To do this, he or she has to be a clever, resourceful, quick-thinking person, able to act at a moment's notice. A spy must be able to remember all kinds of complicated codes and messages, and to disguise himself or herself so as to be completely unrecognizable.

Spies who work for governments to find out political or military secrets are called political spies, while those employed by

Everyone's favourite spy – James Bond.
The notorious Mata Hari.

companies to find out what their rivals are up to are called industrial spies. But spying can be done at all levels. You might spy on a friend to check on his or her training tactics in tennis, for example, in the hope of discovering why the friend always beats you. You may want to spy on a member of a rival gang, to discover whether he or she is planning to do something which will harm *your* gang. Nosy people spy on their neighbours to find out what kind of lives they lead. Someone who cheats in exams is a bit of a spy, too, for they are stealing information from someone else's paper to get the right answer themselves. It's all a far cry from James Bond.

But, of course, spies of the James Bond type do exist in real life. Here are some of the most famous twentieth-century spies.

'Garbo' 'Garbo' was a brilliant double agent. Working from Lisbon in Portugal, with very little knowledge of England, he fed the Germans a series of false reports about troop movements, and invented an entire team of assistants scattered around Britain. His reports entirely deceived the Germans who considered him to be their top agent in Britain, and recommended him for the Iron Cross, a decoration very rarely given to a foreigner.

'La Marchesa' was an elderly Italian noblewoman whose much-loved country estate was commandeered by the Germans in World War II and turned into a communications centre. An accidental meeting with a wounded American serviceman led to her helping to organize partisan groups in Italy. Under the very nose of the German officers billeted in her house she smuggled agents in and out, and set up a communications network of her own to eavesdrop on the enemy. When the Allies landed at Salerno in September 1943 she realized that the centre in her house was the key to the organization of the enemy defences, and she told the Allies to bomb her beloved home.

Lord Baden Powell The founder of the Boy Scouts was a spy during World War 1. Posing as an entomologist studying butterflies, he drew detailed plans of enemy fortifications hidden in intricate drawings of butterflies' wings.

Peter and Helen Kroger The Krogers became headline news in the 1960s. An apparently pleasant, ordinary middle-aged couple living in a bungalow in the London suburb of Ruislip, they were discovered to be extremely competent Soviet spies. The space under the floorboards of their bungalow was found to be packed with special radio equipment, a number of cameras and special photographic equipment and materials, and a microdot reader hidden in a talcum-powder tin.

The Krogers were sentenced to twenty years' imprisonment, but were exchanged for Gerald Brooke, a Briton arrested in the Soviet Union on suspicion of espionage.

Gary Powers Francis Gary Powers was a US Air Force pilot who worked for the CIA. He piloted a very fast spy plane, called the U2, over Russia. The plane contained photographic equipment capable of reproducing fine detail at ground level from a height of 12 000 metres (40 000 feet). Powers' plane was shot down on 1 May 1960 and he was sentenced to ten years' imprisonment. After serving seventeen months, he was exchanged for Colonel Rudolf Abel.

Gary Powers was exchanged for Colonel Rudolf Abel on the Glienicke Bridge, between East and West Berlin.

A resourceful spy will discover lots of ways of spying on a rival gang without being suspected.

CODES AND CIPHERS 1

Do you know the difference between a code and a cipher?

A keen spy will seize any opportunity to decipher his codes.

A code uses a word, a number, a letter, or a symbol to represent a word or group of words. A cipher has a different letter, number, or symbol for each letter in the alphabet. A code requires the use of a code book in which the code words and their meanings are given. This is a disadvantage because the book could fall into the wrong hands, but an advantage because, without the book, the code is indecipherable. A cipher does not require a 'key' as long as its users are aware of which cipher is being used. But its disadvantage is that it can often be cracked by those experienced in code-breaking.

CREATING A CODE

If you want to devise a secret code which no-one but the members of your group will understand, you need first to know roughly what kind of messages you are likely to want to transmit. For example, if you were a political spy, you would want to send messages about movements of ships and aircraft, of visits by politicians to foreign countries, and so on. If you were an industrial spy, you would be more concerned with methods of manufacture, materials, and movement of goods. Either way, you create a code word.

Suppose you were a spy for a company making television sets. You might want to send a message like this: *Latest Japanese model features remote-control video link*. And you might transcribe it like this: *Carrots teacup lawnmower flower apple*. *Carrots* means 'latest Japanese model', *teacup* means 'features', *lawnmower* means 'remote-control', *flower* means 'video' and *apple* means 'link'. Each person who will use the code keeps a code book in which the words and their meanings are listed and can be looked up to decipher messages and to send new ones.

MAKING A CIPHER WHEEL

Here's how to make a device which will give you lots of different options for creating ciphers. You will need some thin card, a pair of compasses, a pencil or pen, and a paper fastener.

1 Using the compasses, or by drawing round the rim of a cup and a saucer, make two circles of card, one about 10 centimetres (4 inches) in diameter and one about 7 centimetres (2¾ inches). Cut them out carefully.

2 Mark the circles as shown in the illustration. The larger disc is lettered and numbered in a clockwise direction; the smaller one is lettered anticlockwise.

3 Make a small hole in the centre of both discs and push a paper fastener through it to hold both discs together yet allow one to revolve upon the other.

4 The cipher wheel is now ready for use. Before you can use it, you need a key letter. Let us suppose it is S.

5 Turn the larger wheel so that its S is opposite the letter A on the smaller wheel. Then you can create the code by using the letters on the smaller wheel as the 'real' ones, and the letters or numbers on the larger wheel as the ciphers.

Here is an example. Using S as the key letter, the word 'contact' can be made into a cipher as Q E F Z S Q Z or as 17 5 6 26 19 17 26.

Make your own code wheel using a plan like this. The smaller wheel inside can be revolved in either direction.

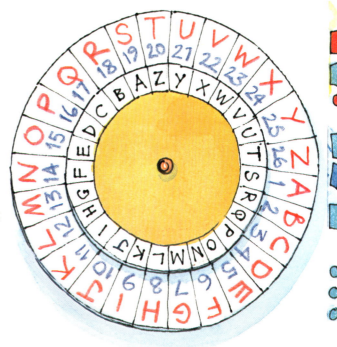

Each person involved in using the cipher will need to make his or her own wheel, and can then be sent any message provided the key letter is given, usually at the beginning of the message.

What does the message below say?
(D) WDIZ YJQ BMZDKVQX BPAZL

Answer on page 32

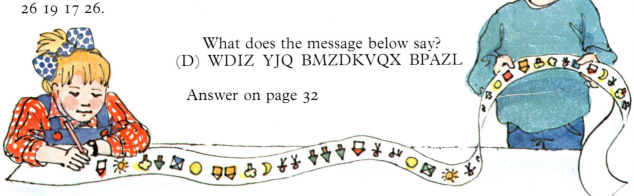

CREATING A DISGUISE

If you want to be a successful spy, able to carry out your activities without being recognized, you have to create a disguise. The best ways of doing this are by disguising your body and your face.

DISGUISING YOUR BODY

Clothing You may think it is impossible to make yourself into an entirely different shape but, with a little ingenuity, it can be done easily.

First of all, you need to borrow an old and preferably over-large coat, such as an old raincoat. You can then make yourself look fatter by strapping a cushion or a pillow round your middle, underneath the coat, and you can make yourself look taller by putting a rolled-up towel or sweater around the back of your neck and shoulders. If you are a girl, you can make yourself appear taller by wearing high-heeled shoes.

It is, of course, more difficult to make yourself look thinner or smaller, but a large, loose coat will hide your weight, and walking with a stoop will make you look shorter.

Movement Next, you have to learn to disguise your movements and mannerisms. If you are right-handed, try to do things with your left hand (and vice-versa), especially if you are being watched.

Then you must disguise your walk. If you normally walk quickly, cultivate a leisurely stroll; if you normally walk slowly, try to hurry a bit. Swing your arms as you go along, and carry an um-

Right: Alec Guinness as John le Carré's spy, George Smiley.

Below left: Make sure you can walk in high-heeled shoes!

ACTING A PART

With a few 'props', you can act out a part which might make it easier for you to gain access to certain places. For example, if you have, or can borrow, a track suit, you can wear your plimsolls or training shoes, tie a band round your hair, and pretend to be a jogger. Carrying a bucket and a cloth, you could be cleaning cars, which gives you an opportunity to linger without being noticed. Wearing an old overall and carrying a broom you could be a road-sweeper, which also means that you can lurk and keep watch on someone. If you can get hold of a collection of really threadbare old clothes, tie a piece of string round your middle and settle down for a snooze in a doorway with your hat pulled over your eyes like an old tramp. But, of course, you won't really be asleep, you'll be keeping a careful ear and eye on everything that goes on.

brella, or a newspaper, or a briefcase, especially if you don't usually do so. Why not adopt a special limp or a stiff leg? So you do it properly, and don't forget which leg to limp with, or which one is stiff, put a pebble in one shoe to make you limp (you'll have to, it will hurt!) and tie a ruler (not too tightly) to the back of your knee with a scarf, handkerchief, or bandage so you can't bend it.

Changing sex If you want to appear to be of the opposite sex, then fasten your coat the other way round and, if the fasteners won't work that way, wrap the coat round and hold it with a belt. Try to walk with shorter steps if you want to appear to be a girl, and with longer ones if you want to appear to be a boy.

Disguised as a newspaper reporter or a market researcher you can use a tape recorder without arousing suspicion.

DISGUISING YOUR FACE

A face mask will hide your identity, but it may draw attention to you! Use a magazine for cutting out faces to fit you.

Two very good 'props' for making your face look completely different are a hat and a pair of dark glasses. If you tuck all your hair under a hat and pull it well down, you will look completely different. You can change your appearance further by folding the brim back, or wearing the hat on one side. A pair of dark glasses is a wonderful disguise, as every film star knows. If you want to look sinister, buy a pair with reflecting lenses so people cannot see your eyes.

Hair Your facial appearance can be changed a lot by changing your hair style. Part your hair in a different place; comb a fringe back or to one side; or, if you don't normally have a fringe then brush your hair forward to create one. If your hair is difficult to persuade to stay in a different style, then wet it first, or borrow some hair spray to hold it in place.

You can make yourself look older by rubbing talcum powder into your hair around the temples – then you'll look as if you're going grey.

If you are a girl and have longish hair, there are lots of ways of changing your appearance. You can hide it all under a hat or scarf; put it up in a bun; plait it; or create lots of different styles using clips and slides.

If you can borrow a wig or hairpiece, that would be splendid but, even if you can't, you might be able to buy some cheap crêpe hair from a joke shop. With it, you can have fun creating bushy eyebrows, beards, moustaches, or long hair sticking out from under your hat.

Make sure you are wearing the right disguise at the right time!

If you are trying to look like a man, rub some of the pencil or shadow around your chin, cheeks, and upper lip to create an unshaven appearance.

If you are trying to look like a glamorous and sophisticated woman, and you have access to make-up, you can try all of it, putting eye shadow on your eyelids, mascara on your eye lashes, powder on your face, blusher on your cheeks, and vivid lipstick on your lips, but take care. It takes a bit of practice to put on make-up properly and, if you go out with your lipstick all smudged and your eye make-up running, you will attract unnecessary attention, and spoil your carefully prepared disguise.

Make-up Theatrical make-up is ideal to create a really effective disguise, but there are other things you can resort to. You can make your skin look suntanned by rubbing a little cocoa powder on it, or you can make yourself look pale by rubbing talcum powder on your face.

If you can borrow some real make-up (do ask permission first), you can have a great time. An eye pencil or some eye shadow in grey or brown can be used to make you look older. Frown in front of a mirror and, where the creases appear across your forehead and at the sides of your mouth, draw in lines with the pencil or shadow. You will look years older!

PLACES FROM WHICH TO SPY

When you have your disguise organized, it's time to go out and do a bit of spying! Here are some suggestions for good places to hide, both indoors and out of doors. Don't forget to take with you a notebook and a pencil, and to allow yourself room in your hiding place to write.

OUT OF DOORS

Up a tree If you can climb a tree and hide in the branches, you will find it is an excellent place for watching and listening to whatever is going on below. But do take care when climbing trees. Don't go too high, or edge out along a branch that may not hold your weight. A good spy only uses hiding-places where he or she will be safe. Of course, if the tree is large enough, you may be able to hide *behind* it, but this could be difficult if the people on whom you are spying are likely to move around much.

Behind a dustbin If you crouch down and make yourself very small you may be able to hide without being seen. If you're very determined, you may even be able to hide *in* the dustbin, but only do this if it is empty and reasonably clean!

You may also be able to hide in a hedge, behind a pillar box, in a telephone box, or among a queue at a bus stop.

You can also 'hide' out in the open. A person sitting on a park bench reading a newspaper is seldom worth a second glance.

Pretending to be birdwatching can be a good way of spying, allowing you to use binoculars without arousing suspicion. Wearing a camouflage head-dress will help your disguise. Make one using a head-band with feathers and twigs, as shown opposite.

INDOORS

If you know where a secret meeting is going to take place, you may be able to hide yourself in the room before the others arrive.

Behind the curtains Full-length curtains make very good hiding-places. But take care that someone isn't likely to draw

the curtains halfway through the meeting and reveal you (for example, if the meeting takes place just before it gets dark). Also make sure your toes don't stick out below the curtains. If the curtains are not full length, you may be able to lie on the windowsill behind them. Take a cushion, you may be there a long time.

Under the furniture You may be able to hide under a table, a sideboard, or a bed, if you are sure the meeting will take place in that room. Any table that has a long cloth covering it makes an excellent hiding place.

In a cupboard or wardrobe This also makes an ideal hiding-place. Pull the door to, but leave a tiny crack so you can hear what is happening, and also to allow you to breathe!

   If you arrive late, and cannot conceal yourself in any of these places in time, then hide behind the door, and either leave before the people in the room do, or flatten yourself against the wall when the door opens so people can come out and not see you.

CODES AND CIPHERS 2

A S
B T
C U
D V
E W
F X
G Y
H Z
I 1
J 2
K 3
L 4
M 5
N 6
O 7
P 8
Q 9
R 10

A •— S •••
B —••• T —
C —•—• U ••—
D —•• V •••—
E • W •——
F ••—• X —••—
G ——• Y —•——
H •••• Z ——••
I •• 1 •————
J •——— 2 ••———
K —•— 3 •••——
L •—•• 4 ••••—
M —— 5 •••••
N —• 6 —••••
O ——— 7 ——•••
P •——• 8 ———••
Q ——•— 9 ————•
R •—• 10 —————

Can you work out what the message above says? Answer on page 32.

When Morse is tapped out on pipes, remember it may well be heard by someone other than your contact!

MORSE CODE

Morse code is perhaps the best-known code in the world. In fact, it is not a code at all, but a cipher. It was created in the nineteenth century by the American inventor of the telegraph system, Samuel Finley Breese Morse, and it uses a system of dots and dashes to represent letters and numbers. The picture above right shows the standard form of Morse code; on the left is an alternative way of representing it.

Morse can be transmitted in a number of ways. In the days of the telegraph, it was tapped out, using long and short taps. It is often flashed with a signalling lamp, and can even be played as music, by someone who is very clever.

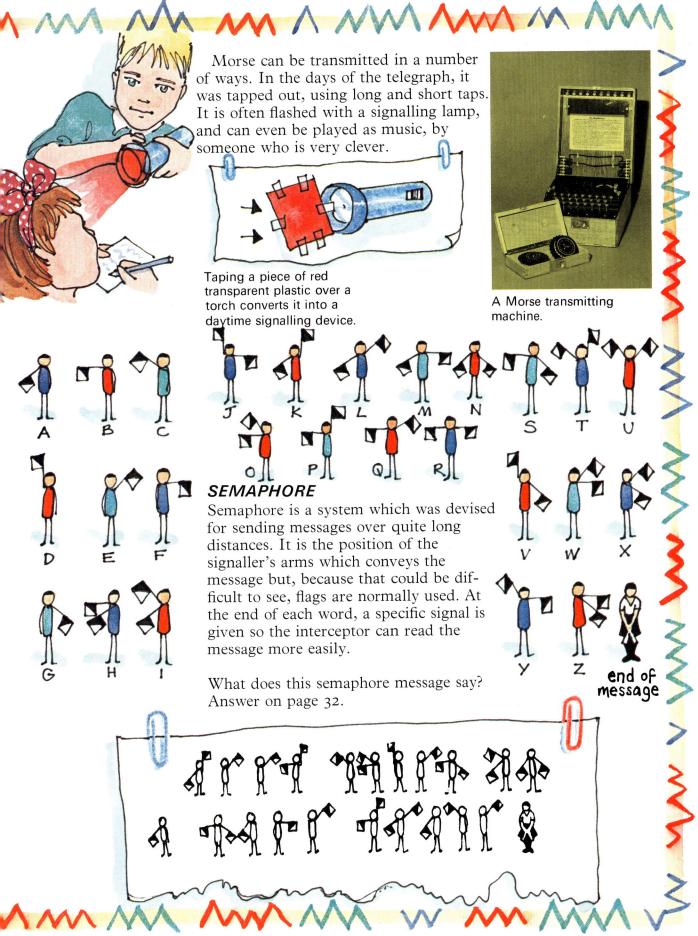

Taping a piece of red transparent plastic over a torch converts it into a daytime signalling device.

A Morse transmitting machine.

SEMAPHORE

Semaphore is a system which was devised for sending messages over quite long distances. It is the position of the signaller's arms which conveys the message but, because that could be difficult to see, flags are normally used. At the end of each word, a specific signal is given so the interceptor can read the message more easily.

What does this semaphore message say? Answer on page 32.

INVISIBLE MESSAGES

When you have to pass a message to a contact you may well write it in a code or cipher, but to make it extra-specially secret, you should write it in invisible ink. Then it can only be read by the person for whom it was intended because anyone coming across it accidentally will never know it is there.

HOW TO MAKE INVISIBLE INK

Substances which can be used as invisible ink are found in every home. Almost any sugar solution – this means sugar dissolved in water – works well. About a teaspoonful of sugar in a glass of water is what you need. You can also try dissolving a teaspoonful of clear honey in a glass of warm water. Ordinary canned or bottled fizzy drinks work, too, because they contain sugar.

Fruit juices also make good invisible ink. The best kinds to use are orange, lemon, and grapefruit juices, which can either be squeezed out of the fruits or used from a bottle or carton. Apple juice works, too, but not quite as well as the others.

Milk makes good ink, too. It is best if it is not too creamy, or you may get greasy marks on the paper, which will give the game away. Neat vinegar works, and a teaspoonful of salt dissolved in a glass of water does too.

If you cannot find any of these things, cut a potato or an onion in half and scrape your 'pen' along the vegetable's surface to collect the juice.

HOW TO WRITE INVISIBLE MESSAGES

Before you can write a message, you need a 'pen'. You cannot use a real pen or pencil, or you will mark the paper, but

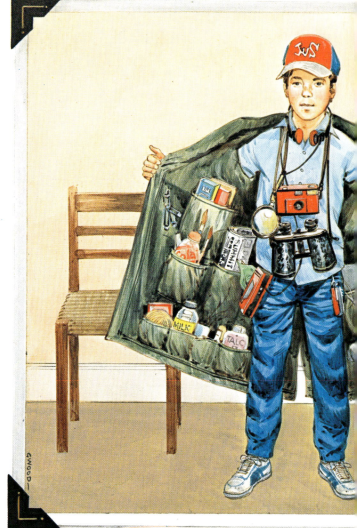

Concealing the tools of your trade is essential for a good spy. Containers and equipment for writing messages should be with you.

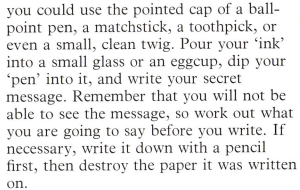

you could use the pointed cap of a ball-point pen, a matchstick, a toothpick, or even a small, clean twig. Pour your 'ink' into a small glass or an eggcup, dip your 'pen' into it, and write your secret message. Remember that you will not be able to see the message, so work out what you are going to say before you write. If necessary, write it down with a pencil first, then destroy the paper it was written on.

As an extra precaution, send your message on the back of a perfectly ordinary letter, or even on a birthday card. This is to prevent suspicion if it is intercepted. A piece of blank paper looks very suspicious!

You can also write a message with a piece of candle, although this has the disadvantage that it can be felt if you rub a finger over the paper.

HOW TO READ INVISIBLE MESSAGES

If the message is written with a candle, it can be made to appear by dusting the paper lightly with talcum powder or flour. The powder will stick to the message but not to the paper. Or you can rub a waxed crayon over it, or paint over the paper with water colour. The crayon or paint will stick to the paper but not to the wax and so the message will be revealed.

If you have written the message in invisible ink, then it can be made to appear by warming the paper. You must do this very carefully so that you don't set fire to it, for this would destroy the message as well as burning you! So warm it by holding it near a lighted bulb in a lamp, or near a central-heating radiator. *Never* hold the paper near a naked flame, a gas or electric cooker, a gas fire, or a radiant electric fire.

Once the paper has been warmed, the message will appear as light-brown writing. It cannot be made to vanish again so, when you have read the message, you will have to destroy the paper.

HIDING PAPERS AND EQUIPMENT

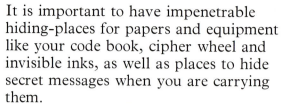

It is important to have impenetrable hiding-places for papers and equipment like your code book, cipher wheel and invisible inks, as well as places to hide secret messages when you are carrying them.

IN YOUR ROOM

Furnishings Papers can be taped to the undersides of tables and sideboards, hidden under mattresses and sofa cushions, and taped to the undersides of drawers. If drawers are taken right out, small objects can be hidden in the space at the back, and the drawer replaced. Take care, though, that the drawer does not stick out and draw attention to it.

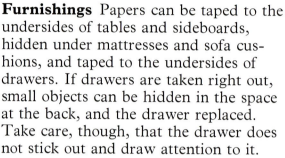

The kinds of large old clocks with removable backs make good hiding-places for small objects. If you are lucky enough to have a grandfather clock, you may be able to keep all kinds of things in it! Magnifying glasses and other small objects can be slipped into empty vases, jugs, and small ornaments.

Pictures make good hiding-places for papers. If possible, remove the back and slip the paper between the picture and the backing sheet but, if this is not possible, then tape the paper to the back of the picture. Papers can also be slipped under the carpet, or under a rug – good hiding-places if you have to act quickly.

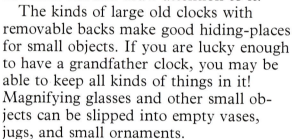

Creating special hiding-places Old books that don't matter too much, such as old annuals, make very good hiding-places. Stick two pages together with adhesive tape along the bottom and side to make a pocket in which to slip a document. If you are willing to sacrifice the book completely, then cut out a central square from most of the pages to make a hiding-place for a cassette, a roll of film, or even a tiny camera.

A Dutch 2½ guilder piece used in World War I for passing messages across the frontier between the Netherlands and the German-occupied part of Belgium.

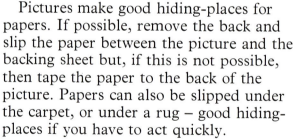

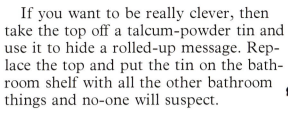

If you want to be really clever, then take the top off a talcum-powder tin and use it to hide a rolled-up message. Replace the top and put the tin on the bathroom shelf with all the other bathroom things and no-one will suspect.

CARRYING SECRET DOCUMENTS

If you are carrying secret documents to a meeting, or to hide them in a dead letterbox (*see* page 22), you may need to conceal them in case you are intercepted by an enemy. Here are some good ways of doing so.

On your clothes Messages, maps, and so on can sometimes be written on your clothes where no-one will think of looking. Use a washable felt-tipped pen, and write on the underside of your socks, on an old handkerchief or scarf, or on the inside of a tie or a pair of gloves. If you are clever, you will disguise the message by using pens of different colours to create a pattern, so it appears to be part of the clothing's design.

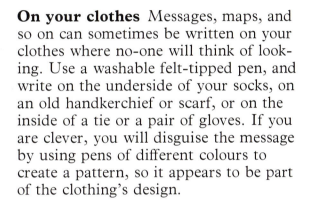

In your clothes Messages can be pushed inside a tie, hidden in your sock, or concealed in your gloves. If you use gloves, take care that the message stays in the glove when you take it off.

If you are prepared to take time and trouble, you can make a false pocket lining with which to fool everyone. Use a scrap of old material, fold it over, and stitch it along two sides to make a pocket shape slightly smaller than your real pocket. Stitch or safety pin it inside your real pocket, taking care that its top edge cannot be seen. Hide the message underneath the false pocket, and put your handkerchief, bus ticket, toffees, and so on in the false pocket so that, if someone searches you, they will not be suspicious.

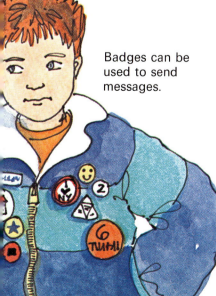

Badges can be used to send messages.

MAKING CONTACT

There are a number of ways in which you can pass a message to a contact without being detected by the enemy.

MEETING IN THE STREET

If the meeting is to be a casual encounter in the street, outside a shop, or at a bus stop, then the simplest way to pass a message is simply to bump into your contact 'accidentally' and pass him or her a slip of paper as you do so.

If you think this method might be spotted too easily, then both you and your contact should carry identical bags, parcels, or umbrellas. Before you set out, you hide the message in whatever you are carrying and, when you meet your contact, you bump into each other as before, but you both drop your bags. Amid the confusion and apologies that follow, each picks up the other's bag, so the message is safely transferred to the contact.

MEETING IN A PARK

A park bench makes a good meeting place. Stroll into the park carrying a newspaper in which the message is hidden. Sit on a bench and casually read your paper, making sure the message does not fall out. Your contact arrives, and sits at the other end of the bench. Without apparently noticing him or her, get up and walk away, leaving the paper behind. The contact can then pick it up and read it, and eventually go off with the message.

If one of you has a dog, then the message can be attached to its collar. The other person, under the guise of patting the dog, can either take the message or leave it there attached to the collar.

Another way is to hide your message inside the wrapper of a chocolate bar. Eat the bar, and then throw the wrapper, complete with message, into a litter bin. The contact can then come along and retrieve it.

If there is an ice-cream van in the park, then a really clever method that no-one will suspect can be used. The message should either be written on greaseproof paper or carefully sealed in a polythene bag. It is then pushed into the centre of an ice-cream cornet, which the spy carefully hands to the contact as if kindly buying him or her an ice-cream.

MEETING ON A BUS OR TRAIN

The contact should already be on the bus when you get on. You sit down and tuck the message down the side of the seat and, after only one or two stops, get off the bus. The contact will then move into your seat and retrieve the message. The contact should not get off the bus immediately to avoid arousing suspicion in anyone watching.

MEETING AT A SPORTS CENTRE

If you are playing a ball game, then the message can be stuck to the ball and passed to the opponent. If playing badminton, it can be hidden inside a shuttlecock.

No-one will suspect you of passing a message in a swimming pool, but you can if you are a good swimmer. Write the message in indelible ink, wrap it carefully in polythene, tuck it into your swimming costume, and then take it out and pass it to your contact *underwater*. No matter how carefully you are being watched, no-one will detect this!

MEETING IN A RESTAURANT

A restaurant is an obvious meeting place, so you have to be extremely careful. You can pass a message under the table, slide it under the table-cloth to be retrieved later, or pass it with the salt or the sugar. You should always pretend that your contact is a complete stranger.

Messages can be slipped inside library books to be picked up by a contact, but it is a risky business because they could easily fall into the wrong hands!

SUBSTITUTION CIPHERS

Substitution ciphers are simple ciphers in which another letter, or a number, is substituted for the 'real' letter of the alphabet. Here are some examples:

real letters	cipher letters	cipher numbers	Caesar's cipher
A	Z	1	D
B	Y	2	E
C	X	3	F
D	W	4	G
E	V	5	H
F	U	6	I
G	T	7	J
H	S	8	K
I	R	9	L
J	Q	10	M
K	P	11	N
L	O	12	O
M	N	13	P
N	M	14	Q
O	L	15	R
P	K	16	S
Q	J	17	T
R	I	18	U
S	H	19	V
T	G	20	W
U	F	21	X
V	E	22	Y
W	D	23	Z
X	C	24	A
Y	B	25	B
Z	A	26	C

As you can see, for the purpose of working out these ciphers, the alphabet is assumed to start again at A once you have passed Z.

The first two ciphers above are very simple, and would be easy to crack. But a number cipher could be made to appear very complicated if, instead of starting with A = 1, you started with A = 73, or even 273, for example. Or you could create a cipher using only odd or only even numbers, or prime numbers.

Caesar's cipher is that used by the Roman emperor, Julius Caesar, who lived from about 102 to 44 BC, to communicate with his troops. There's nothing new about ciphers!

BOX CIPHER

In a box cipher, the message is written up or down a box grid. Suppose your message is: 'Meet A at zoo Wednesday p.m.' You write it out like this:

M	S	W	A	M
X	D	E	T	E
J	A	D	Z	E
L	Y	N	O	T
B	P	E	O	A

In this example, the message starts in the top right-hand corner of the grid and reads down the right-hand column, then down the column next to it, and so on, until the message is finished. The extra letters after the message are called 'nulls', and are just there to fill up the grid.

To make this cipher even more confusing, read the grid across and write it out as words like this:

Mswam Xdete
Jadze Lynot
Bpeoa.

RAIL FENCE CIPHER

This cipher involves writing out a message on two lines, one above the other. For example, the message PAT ARRIVING PADDINGTON STATION NOON FRIDAY is written like this:

```
P T R I I G A D N T N T T O N O F I A
A A R V N P D I G O S A I N O N R D Y
```

Then all the top letters are written out consecutively, followed by all the lower letters, like this:

PTRIIGADNTNTTONOFIAAARVNPDIGOSAINONRDY

These letters are then arbitrarily divided into groups to look like words:

PTRIIG ADNTNT TONOF IAAARVNP DIGO SAINON RDY

MSWAM XDETE JADZE LYNOT BPEOA

The result looks very difficult to decipher but, of course, all you do is ignore the letter groupings and write the message out on two lines as before. It is important to remember that the message should be made up of an even number of letters.

ROSICRUCIAN CIPHER

This ingenious cipher is based on one constructed in the sixteenth century by an Italian called Giovanni Porta. Again, the finished cipher looks very complicated, but it is based on the following grids:

A	B	C		J
D	E	F	K	L
G	H	I		M

N	O	P		W
Q	R	S	X	Y
T	U	V		Z

Thus A= ⌐, B=⊔, C=⌐, J=∨, K=>, N=⌐, O=⊔, and so on.

What does the following message say? Answer on page 32

DEAD LETTERBOXES

A dead letterbox is a spy's name for a place where a message can be left to be picked up by a contact later. It has to be a place no-one will suspect, and a place where the message will be safe from accidental discovery by a passer-by.

IN GARDENS, PARKS, AND PLAYGROUNDS

The traditional dead letterbox is an old hollow tree, and there may well be one of these on one of your regular routes. Make sure the message is well tucked into the cavity so it will not be spotted by prying eyes.

In a park or garden where there are flowerbeds, the message can be wrapped in polythene and hidden in the earth near a particular flower. Or it can be hidden under a large stone, or under gravel, as long as it will be possible for the contact to find the hiding-place quickly.

A message can also be taped to the underside of a park bench or swing seat, or to the underside of another piece of play equipment. Under the lower end of a slide is a good place, for everyone will be too busy looking upwards at people on the slide to notice it.

ON A BEACH

Again, wrap the message in polythene and bury it under a sand castle. Make sure the castle is above the high-water mark or it will disappear, taking the message with it.

IN A RESTAURANT

Tape the message to the underside of the sugar bowl or mustard pot, or simply leave it under the tablecloth. It could even be attached to the back of an old bill and left under a plate.

AROUND YOUR HOUSE

If you don't mind your contact being seen at your house (and it may be all right as long as he or she is not seen meeting you there), you can leave a message under the door mat, inside an empty milk bottle (so it looks like a note for the milkman, but take care that the milkman doesn't arrive before the contact), or taped to the under-side of a window sill.

IN A CINEMA

This is a bit more complicated, but it's a good way of avoiding suspicion. You and the contact both buy tickets for the same seat in the cinema, for different showings of the film. Or, if your cinema does not sell numbered tickets, you both agree to sit in the same seat, say G4. You go to the earlier showing and leave the message tucked down the seat, or taped to the back of it, or under the armrest, and your contact goes to the next showing of the film and retrieves it.

DISGUISING YOUR VOICE

Learning how to disguise your voice is an important part of creating a really effective disguise, for it is no use looking completely different if your voice gives you away. Here are some ways of doing it. They all take a little practice and, if you have access to a tape or cassette recorder, and you can try out your new voice in private before using it in public, you will find it a great help.

ON THE TELEPHONE

It is easier to disguise your voice on the telephone than when you are face to face with someone because they cannot see what contortions you are making.

1 Put your tongue behind your lower front teeth when you speak. You will develop a lisp!

4 Try speaking with your thumb or a finger in your mouth.

2 Hold your nose between your thumb and first finger to make your voice sound as if you suffer from swollen adenoids. The tighter you hold it, the more pronounced will be the effect.

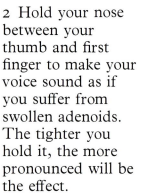
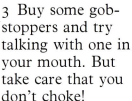

3 Buy some gobstoppers and try talking with one in your mouth. But take care that you don't choke!

5 Spread a cotton handkerchief over the mouthpiece of the phone and speak through that.

6 Tie a large handkerchief or a scarf round your face to cover your nose and mouth so you look like a bandit, and speak through it.

In addition, when speaking on the telephone, you can try out some of the ploys listed.

IN PERSON

Before you try out a new voice, make sure you have decided exactly how you are going to disguise it. Once you have decided, do not change your disguise. Otherwise you will sound most peculiar!

If you are being watched, you can try talking out of the side of your mouth.

1 Change the speed at which you speak. Some people naturally speak much more quickly than others so, if you normally speak quickly, try to speak slowly in your new voice and, if you normally speak slowly, then try to speed up.

2 Similarly, try to alter the pitch of your voice, that is, make it sound higher or lower than usual.

3 Cultivate an accent. This is difficult to do and requires lots of practice, but you can try to talk like someone from Scotland, Wales, Ireland, Australia, the southern United States or the Far East. If you want to be convincing, don't overdo it. A Scots accent with someone saying, 'Hoots, mon', all the time will just give you away!

MESSAGES WITHOUT WORDS

It is possible to pass a message on to someone without using any words at all, provided you can see each other. You may wonder how, and the answer is by using your clothes and the movements of your body.

To do this successfully, you need to have an agreed code between yourself and the person or persons to whom you are passing the message. You decide that certain types and colours of clothing, and certain bodily actions, such as blowing your nose or scratching your head, have specific meanings. You can give them any meanings you like as long as each of you knows for certain what they are. Here are some examples.

MOVEMENT MESSAGES

scratching your head	*means*	yes
scratching your nose	*means*	no
blowing your nose	*means*	definitely not
a cough	*means*	danger, look out
blinking your eyes very rapidly in succession	*means*	the enemy approaches
standing or sitting with your right leg crossed over the left	*means*	don't tell anyone what you know
standing or sitting with your left leg crossed over the right	*means*	tell them a false story to mislead them
rubbing your chin	*means*	leave as soon as possible

pulling at your ear	*means*	let me sort out the problem
rubbing your eye	*means*	I am in great danger, help me

You can indicate numbers by folding your arms and leaving a certain number of fingers showing.

CLOTHING MESSAGES

One of the simplest ways of passing a message via your clothing is to use a colour code. Again, you have to have a pre-arranged set of signals with your contacts, but they might work something like the list below. If you don't have a sweater or a dress of the right colour, then something small like a tie, a scarf, a belt, or even a badge, would do.

blue	*means*	danger
yellow	*means*	all clear
white	*means*	time for attack
red	*means*	the suspect must be followed
green	*means*	the operation is going well
black	*means*	they suspect us, take great care

The colour messages above were chosen deliberately to be confusing. For example, red normally means 'danger' and green 'all clear', but in case anyone suspects, it is better to give them a different meaning.

You can also use the type of clothes you wear to pass on a message. For example, if you wear jeans and a sweatshirt, this could mean 'all is going according to plan', whereas more formal clothing might mean 'we need more help with this project'. Wearing a hat, or not wearing a hat, could indicate a simple 'yes' or 'no' answer to a known question.

Bearing in mind the types of code suggested above, what are James Bond and the boy at the bus stop trying to say? Answers on page 32.

CODES AND CIPHERS 4

MAKING A CODE GRILLE

A code grille is a device which allows you to send a highly secret message concealed within a perfectly ordinary letter. The grille is simply a piece of paper or card with slots cut out of it, which fits over an ordinary letter and therefore allows only certain words to be read through it. You and your contact each needs a grille of the same pattern. You write ordinary letters to each other which contain the words of the secret message, which in turn are revealed by the grille. This is how it works. Look at this ordinary letter:

and then read it with the grille placed over it.

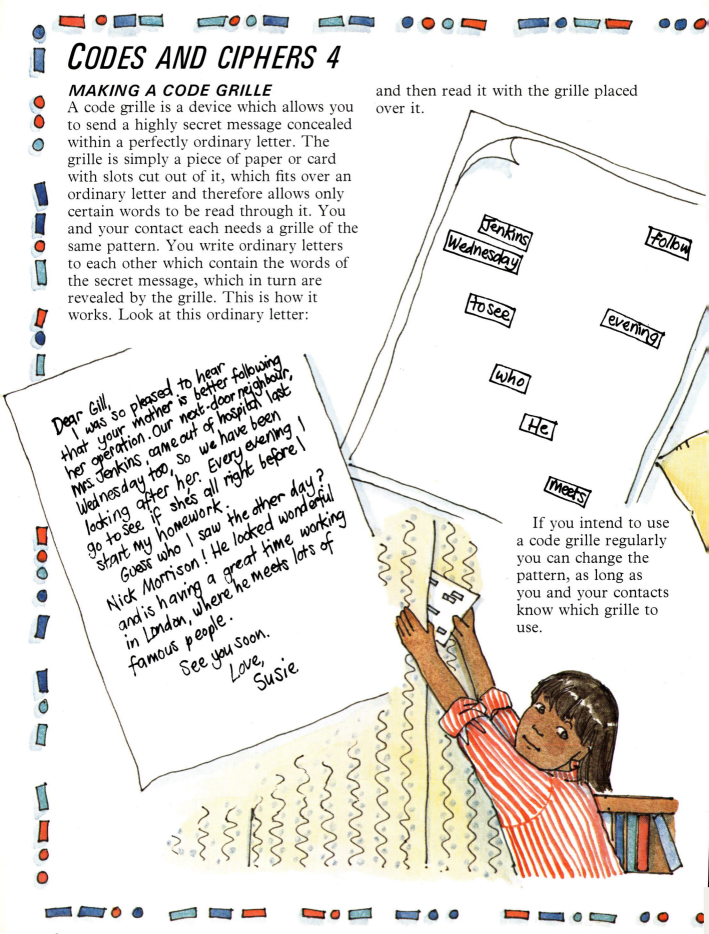

Dear Gill,
I was so pleased to hear that your mother is better following her operation. Our next-door neighbour, Mrs. Jenkins, came out of hospital last Wednesday too, so we have been looking after her. Every evening I go to see if she's all right before I start my homework.
Guess who I saw the other day? Nick Morrison! He looked wonderful and is having a great time working in London, where he meets lots of famous people.
See you soon.
Love,
Susie.

If you intend to use a code grille regularly you can change the pattern, as long as you and your contacts know which grille to use.

PINHOLE CODE

A pinhole code works in a similar way to a code grille in that it allows you to send an ordinary letter, containing a secret message, which will not arouse suspicion. All you do is to mark the words in the code message with tiny pinholes, which will be indistinguishable until the contact holds the letter up to the light. Then the holes will be seen easily and the message can be read.

In the example below, the pinholes have been indicated by small dots.

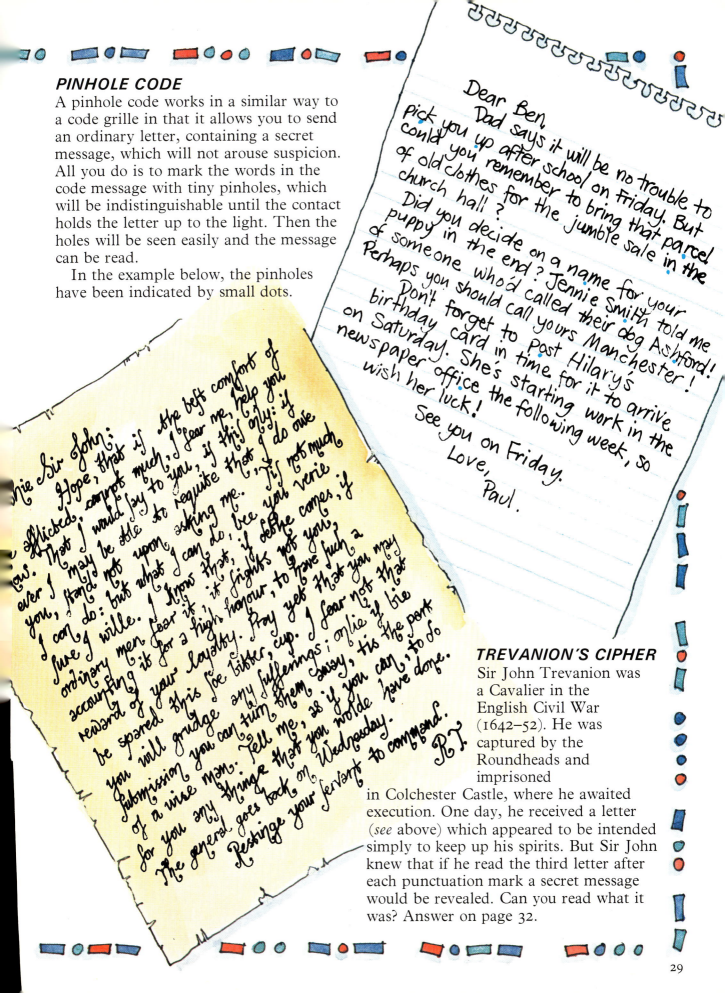

Dear Ben

Dad says it will be no trouble to pick you up after school on Friday. But could you remember to bring that parcel of old clothes for the jumble sale in the church hall?

Did you decide on a name for your puppy in the end? Jennie Smith told me of someone who'd called their dog Ashford! Perhaps you should call yours Manchester!

Don't forget to post Hilary's birthday card in time for it to arrive on Saturday. She's starting work in the newspaper office the following week, so wish her luck!

See you on Friday.

Love,
Paul.

TREVANION'S CIPHER

Sir John Trevanion was a Cavalier in the English Civil War (1642–52). He was captured by the Roundheads and imprisoned in Colchester Castle, where he awaited execution. One day, he received a letter (*see* above) which appeared to be intended simply to keep up his spirits. But Sir John knew that if he read the third letter after each punctuation mark a secret message would be revealed. Can you read what it was? Answer on page 32.

MAKING YOUR ROOM SPY-PROOF

Once you become a spy, you have to be on the alert against enemy spies. They are probably just as anxious to listen to the conversations you have with your contacts and to snoop around your room looking for code books and microfilm as you are to do the same to them!

On pages 16 and 17 you found where you could hide things in your room so they would not be obvious if someone entered. You can also lay a false trail by leaving fake code books and messages around the place to put them off the scent – these are all ways of making your room spy proof. But there are other things you can do, too.

MAKING AN ALARM

If you are in another part of the house or garden and you want an instant warning of anyone entering your room, or if you are holding a meeting in your room and want warning of anyone approaching, you need to make an alarm. All you need are two or three empty drinks cans, a longish piece of string or fine black thread, and two or three large paperclips, used matchsticks, or hair grips.

To make an alarm which will warn you if someone enters your room, cut the string into as many pieces as you have tin cans. To one end of each piece of string attach the large paperclip, used matchstick, or hair grip, by knotting the string firmly around it. Carefully pin the other ends of the string together to the lintel on the outside of the door of your room. Then, by folding it flat back against the string, insert the paperclip, matchstick, or hair grip of each piece into the hole left by the ring-pull section of the can, and twist it round across the hole so that the can is suspended from the string. Then, as soon as someone opens the door, the cans will jangle together and instantly warn you of the interloper's presence.

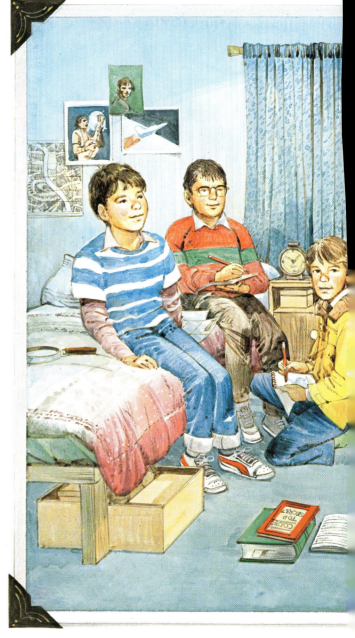

If you want to position the alarm some distance from your room to warn you of someone approaching, you will need the same equipment as described above, but the string should be replaced by fine black cotton. Attach the cotton to the cans in the same way as before, and stretch the cotton, about 4 centimetres (1½ inches) off the ground, across the corridor or other place along which a spy would have to

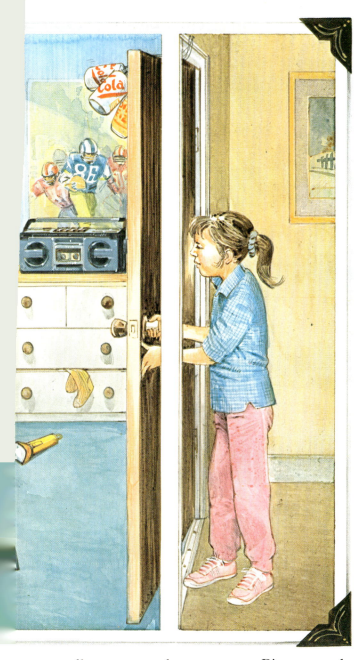

OTHER SECURITY SYSTEMS

If you cannot manage to make an alarm and you want to know if someone has been in your room, there are other things you can do.

First of all, you can stick fine hairs or very thin pieces of thread across the doors of cupboards or across drawers in which you keep your papers and secret equipment. Then, if anyone opens the cupboards or drawers, they will break the hairs or threads, and you will be able to tell at a glance that they have been there.

Then, you can dust for fingerprints. Before you do this it is as well to know what your own fingerprints look like.

Take a clean, polished glass and hold it with all the fingers of your right hand. If your fingertips are not very greasy and do not easily leave prints you could borrow a little hand cream, or rub a little butter on them, before grasping the glass. When you have left a set of prints, wipe your hand clean and carefully brush a little flour or talcum powder over the glass. The prints will be clearly revealed. To file them for future reference, carefully stretch a piece of transparent adhesive tape across them, and then, equally carefully, stick it on a piece of dark-coloured paper or card. Repeat the procedure for your left hand.

Follow the same sequence when you are dusting equipment in your room for the fingerprints of intruders. These, too, can be fixed with powder or flour and stuck on to a card so you can compare them with your own. Once you are sure they are not yours, or those of your contacts, you may be able to find out to whom they belong.

walk to approach your room. Pin one end of the thread to the wall or skirting board, and tuck the cans away in a pile out of sight at the other end of the thread, with it stretched taut. If someone approaches, he or she will trip over the thread and pull down the pile of cans, making a terrible noise and warning you that the person is there.

ANSWERS

Codes and Ciphers 1 Page 5
The message says: 'Have fun creating codes'.

Codes and Ciphers 2 Page 12
The Morse message says: 'All good spies know Morse.'
The semaphore message says: 'Keep codes in a safe place'.

Codes and Ciphers 3 Page 21
The message in Rosicrucian cipher says: 'Club meeting at five in park.'

Messages without Words Page 27
James Bond: 'The suspect must be followed.' The boy at the bus stop: 'Don't tell anyone what you know.'

Codes and Ciphers 4 Page 29
The message to Sir John Trevanion read: 'Panel at east end of chapel slides'. Sir John managed to persuade his jailers to let him go to the chapel to pray, and thus escaped.

Index

Published in 1988 by
The Hamlyn Publishing Group Limited
a division of Paul Hamlyn Publishing
Michelin House, 81 Fulham Road, London SW3 6RB

Copyright © The Hamlyn Publishing Group Limited 1988

ISBN 0 600 55741 3

Printed and bound in Italy
Front jacket illustration: Rachel Stevens
Illustrations: Rachel Stevens, Linda Rogers
Associates (Gerry Wood)
Photographic acknowledgments: Imperial War Museum, Kobal Collection,
Photo Source, Science Library
Design: Jillian Haines
General editors: Gillian Denton, Lynne Williams